Extreme Weather

WILDFIRES

Martha London

DiscoverRoo
An Imprint of Pop!
popbooksonline.com

abdobooks.com

Published by Pop!, a division of ABDO, PO Box 398166, Minneapolis, Minnesota 55439.

Printed in the United States of America, North Mankato, Minnesota.

052019
092019

THIS BOOK CONTAINS RECYCLED MATERIALS

Cover Photo: Shutterstock Images
Interior Photos: Shutterstock Images, 1, 10–11 (fire triangle), 14, 22, 23, 26, 28, 29 (bottom); iStockphoto, 5, 6, 7, 8, 9, 10 (wind), 11 (thermometer), 11 (storm), 10–11 (logs), 10–11 (grass), 13, 15, 19, 25, 27, 29 (fire), 29 (checkmarks), 29 (fire rating), 29 (campfire), 29 (safe and key), 29 (car), 29 (house), 29 (mask), 29 (television), 30; Danny Lawson/PA Wire URN:37279305/Press Association/AP Images, 16–17; Jae C. Hong/AP Images, 20; Cathleen Allison/AP Images, 21; Danny Lawson/PA Wire URN:37279308/Press Association/AP Images, 31

Editor: Connor Stratton
Series Designer: Sophie Geister-Jones

Library of Congress Control Number: 2018965062

Publisher's Cataloging-in-Publication Data

Names: London, Martha, author.

Title: Wildfires / by Martha London.

Description: Minneapolis, Minnesota : Pop!, 2020 | Series: Extreme weather | Includes online resources and index.

Identifiers: ISBN 9781532163982 (lib. bdg.) | ISBN 9781532165429 (ebook)

Subjects: LCSH: Wildfires--Juvenile literature. | Fire weather--Juvenile literature. | Wildfires--United States--Prevention and control--Juvenile literature. | Natural disasters--Juvenile literature.

Classification: DDC 363.34--dc23

WELCOME TO DiscoverRoo!

Pop open this book and you'll find QR codes loaded with information, so you can learn even more!

Scan this code* and others like it while you read, or visit the website below to make this book pop!

popbooksonline.com/wildfires

*Scanning QR codes requires a web-enabled smart device with a QR code reader app and a camera.

TABLE OF CONTENTS

CHAPTER 1

HOW WILDFIRES FORM

A wildfire is a large fire in a natural place. For example, many wildfires occur in forests. The fire's raging flames spread out of control. They feed off dry trees, bushes, and other plants.

WATCH A VIDEO HERE!

Some wildfires have burned areas the size of New York City.

Fires need three things to burn and spread. First, fires need fuel. Fuel is anything that can burn. In a forest, fuel could be leaves, trees, and grass. Second, fires need **oxygen**. Third, fires need a source of heat.

Many wildfires use trees as fuel. For this reason, wildfires are sometimes called forest fires.

Lightning can provide the heat source for a wildfire. But most wildfires are caused by people. For example, people may not fully **extinguish** a campfire. Or a cigarette might be left burning on the ground. But once the fire starts, nature gives it the fuel to spread.

Thoughtless human actions cause a large number of wildfires.

If left unattended, campfires can spread and start wildfires.

DID YOU KNOW?

Wind can carry a single **ember** for miles. That spark can be enough to start a wildfire.

THE FIRE TRIANGLE

Fire needs oxygen, heat, and fuel to start. These three things are often called the fire triangle.

Heat
Fire
Fuel

CHAPTER 2

WHERE WILDFIRES FORM

Certain areas are more likely to have wildfires. These areas are often filled with trees or other plant life. The air in these places is usually dry. And temperatures are hot.

LEARN MORE HERE!

Forests with many dry or dead trees catch fire more easily than wetter forests.

In 2018, four massive wildfires swept through California.

For these reasons, many wildfires occur in the western United States. Wildfires are also common in Australia and central African countries. But wildfires can start anywhere on Earth.

In Australia, wildfires often happen in a dry area called the Outback.

DID YOU KNOW?

In Australia, wildfires are often called bushfires.

In addition, **climate change** is changing where wildfires form. Rising temperatures have made **droughts** more extreme. Dry fuel burns more

Firefighters try to put out a wildfire in the United Kingdom.

easily. As a result, wildfires are becoming more common in more places on Earth.

DID YOU KNOW?

In 2018, more than 55,000 wildfires occurred in the United States.

CHAPTER 3

EFFECTS

A wildfire can burn almost everything in its path. One wildfire can destroy thousands of homes. It can grow to be the size of a large city. And it can last for months at a time. Stopping wildfires can be very difficult.

LEARN MORE HERE!

A wildfire burned the color off a sign in California.

Wildfires can also fill the air with smoke. This smoke has tiny parts of materials that burned in the fire. These parts are dangerous to breathe in. The smoke can cause heart problems. It can also damage people's lungs.

DID YOU KNOW?

Wildfire smoke can affect people who are hundreds of miles away from the fire.

A wildfire in Nevada sends up thick, black smoke.

New plants grow in a forest after a wildfire.

However, not all wildfires are harmful. Wildfires are a natural part of many **ecosystems**. Fires clear old

plant life. New plants can then grow. Some plants even need fire to survive.

THE TREE THAT LOVES FIRE

Lodgepole pine trees need fire to sprout new seeds. These trees keep their seeds trapped in pine cones. The cones burst open only in very high temperatures. A wildfire can create enough heat to split open the cones. When they split, the seeds fall to the ground. After the fire, new lodgepole pine trees can grow.

CHAPTER 4

STAYING SAFE

Wildfires can start suddenly and spread quickly. Communities send out warnings if a wildfire is nearby. Sometimes these fires spread into towns and cities. When that happens, people may need to **evacuate** their homes.

COMPLETE AN ACTIVITY HERE!

People may have just a few minutes to evacuate before a wildfire reaches an area.

People also can protect themselves from wildfire smoke. They wear masks and stay indoors as much as possible. People may close all the doors and windows of one room. Smoky air will be less likely to enter that room.

DID YOU KNOW?

The masks people use during wildfires are called N95 respirators.

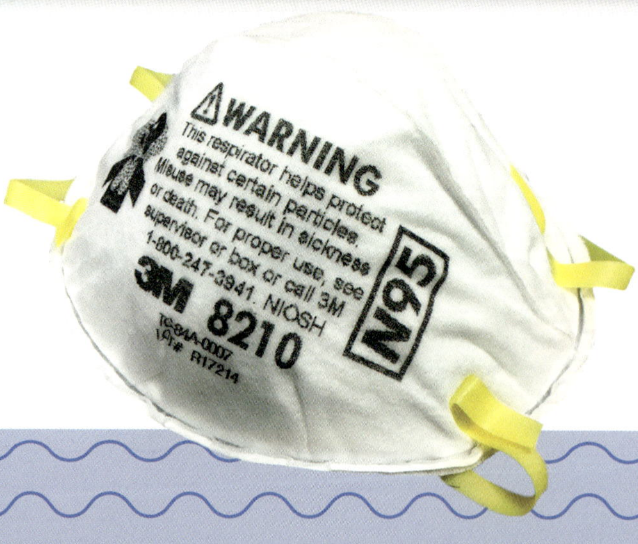

To stop a wildfire from spreading, firefighters sometimes do a controlled burn. In this process, they start small fires on purpose. These fires burn up fuel before the wildfire can. Removing fuel can help prevent future wildfires too.

A firefighter starts a controlled fire.

Many public areas have signs that show the level of fire danger.

The United States has a fire danger rating system as well. This system tells people how likely a wildfire is. When the danger rating is high, people must be extra careful. People can take steps to be safer before, during, or after a wildfire.

Wildfire Safety Checklist

- Check the fire danger rating for your area.
- Make sure campfires are fully put out.
- Keep important items in a fireproof box.
- Evacuate if necessary.
- If there is smoke, stay inside and wear a mask.
- Follow the news for weather updates.

MAKING CONNECTIONS

TEXT-TO-SELF

Are wildfires common where you live? Why or why not?

TEXT-TO-TEXT

Wildfires are more common during droughts. What information about droughts have you read in other books?

TEXT-TO-WORLD

When fire danger ratings are high, people must be extra careful. What are some actions people could take to help keep fires from spreading?

GLOSSARY

climate change – differences in Earth's weather patterns, often including a rising temperature.

drought – a period when the weather is dry.

ecosystem – a group of plants and animals in a natural location.

ember – a small, glowing piece from a fire.

evacuate – to leave a place in order to stay safe.

extinguish – to put out a fire.

oxygen – a gas found in the air, which can catch on fire.

INDEX

ONLINE RESOURCES

popbooksonline.com

Scan this code* and others like it while you read, or visit the website below to make this book pop!

popbooksonline.com/wildfires

*Scanning QR codes requires a web-enabled smart device with a QR code reader app and a camera.